I
BELIEVE

THE NICENE CREED

Illustrated by
Pauline Baynes

EERDMANS BOOKS FOR YOUNG READERS

Grand Rapids, Michigan   Cambridge, U.K.

Bl. Eerd. 4/03   7.20

I Believe: The Nicene Creed copyright © Frances Lincoln Limited 2003
Illustrations copyright © Pauline Baynes 2003

First published in Great Britain in 2003 by
Frances Lincoln Limited, 4 Torriano Mews
Torriano Avenue, London NW5 2RZ
www.franceslincoln.com

This edition published in 2003 under license
from Francis Lincoln Limited
by Eerdmans Books for Young Readers
An imprint of Wm. B. Eerdmans Publishing Co.
255 Jefferson Ave S.E.
Grand Rapids, Michigan 49503
P.O. Box 163 Cambridge CB3 9PU U.K.

www.eerdmans.com/youngreaders

ISBN 0-8028-5258-0

03 04 05 06 07 08   7 6 5 4 3 2 1

A catalog record of this book is available
from The Library of Congress

Set in Hiroshige Book
Printed in Singapore

For Joy Backhouse

I Believe in one God

the Father Almighty,

Maker of heaven and earth,

And of all things visible

and invisible:

And in one Lord Jesus Christ,

the only-begotten Son of God,

Begotten of his Father before

all worlds,

God of God, Light of Light,

Very God of very God,

Begotten, not made,

Being of one substance with the Father,

By whom all things were made:

Who for us men and for our salvation

came down from heaven,

And was incarnate by the Holy Ghost

of the Virgin Mary,

And was made man,

And was crucified also for us

under Pontius Pilate.

He suffered and was buried,

And the third day he rose again

according to the Scriptures,

And ascended into heaven,

And sitteth on the right hand

of the Father.

And he shall come again with glory

to judge both the quick

and the dead:

Whose kingdom shall have

no end.

And I believe in the Holy Ghost,

The Lord and giver of life,

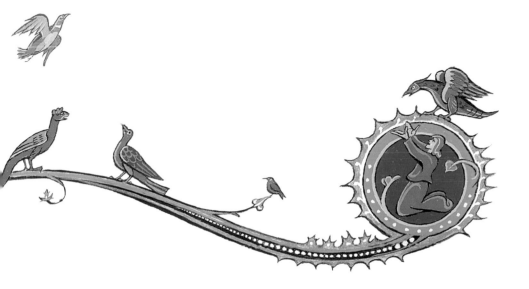

Who proceedeth from the Father

and the Son,

Who with the Father and the Son together

is worshipped and glorified,

Who spake by the Prophets.

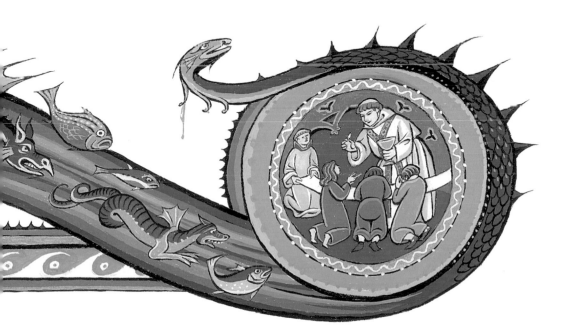

And I believe one Catholic

and Apostolic Church.

I acknowledge one Baptism

for the remission of sins.

And I look for the Resurrection

of the dead,

And the life of the world to come.

Amen

ABOUT THE NICENE CREED

For the first three centuries of its existence, the Christian Church struggled to survive. Threatened by persecution and challenged by other philosophies, it endeavored to adapt the language of the gospels, developed in a Hebraic and Jewish-Christian context, to the surrounding Graeco-Roman world.

In AD 312, Flavius Valerius Constantinus won control of the Roman Empire. Attributing his victory to a dream of Christ the night before the decisive battle, he was converted to Christianity and gave formal recognition to the Christian Church, taking "One God, one Lord, one faith, one church, one empire, one emperor" as his motto.

It soon became clear that the new Church was split by theological disputes, and in AD 325 Constantine convened a council in Nicaea at which a creed — a summary of the articles of Christian faith — was written and signed by most of the bishops. This creed, revised in AD 381, is now known as the Nicene Creed.

One of several early Christian creeds — among them the Apostles' and the Athanasian Creeds — the Nicene Creed is regarded as the most ecumenical, representing the beliefs of more of the Christian world than any other creed. It is used by most Protestant churches, as well as by the Roman Catholic Church, and Eastern Orthodox churches, and remains a rock of Christian belief to this day.